For Peter, Shane, and Quinn—my greatest gifts.
For Mary and my mother, Kay—who taught
me strength in motherhood.—J.Q.N.

To Leah, my love and a most wonderful
mother of my children.—T.L.

ISBN 978-0-545-41543-9

Text copyright © 2008 by Jeannine Q. Norris.
Illustrations copyright © 2008 by Tim Ladwig. All rights reserved.
Published by Scholastic Inc., 557 Broadway, New York, NY 10012, by arrangement
with HarperCollins Children's Books, a division of HarperCollins Publishers.
SCHOLASTIC and associated logos are trademarks and/or
registered trademarks of Scholastic Inc.

12 11 10 9 8 7 6 5 4 3 2   11 12 13 14 15 16/0

Printed in the U.S.A.   40

First Scholastic printing, November 2011

Typography by Rachel Zegar

Tonight
You Are My Baby
Mary's Christmas Gift

Written by **Jeannine Q. Norris**   Illustrated by **Tim Ladwig**

SCHOLASTIC INC.
New York Toronto London Auckland
Sydney Mexico City New Delhi Hong Kong

You are my beautiful gift from God above
And to you I give a mother's forever love.

In this moment I feel what all mothers know—
To hold you close and never want to let go.

Tomorrow you will be King,

But tonight you are my baby. . . .

I marvel at the miracle on this wondrous night—
God's great plan with us, a carpenter and wife.

I was chosen to hold you so close and warm,
Right here with the animals snug in this barn.

I pray for strength as all mothers sometimes do
And try to understand what will be asked of you.

I look for answers in this crystal, chilly night
But only see the one star—which is so very bright.

This star will bring the others and I will start to share.
But tonight you are mine—to give my tender care.

Tomorrow you will be King,

But tonight you are my baby. . . .

As I cradle you gently, the answer is quite clear.
Strength comes from you, my babe, in my arms right here.

For God blessed me with this quiet winter night,
As I am the first to see that you are the Light.

I kiss your tiny fingers and little perfect head,
Lay you in the manger that tonight will be your bed.

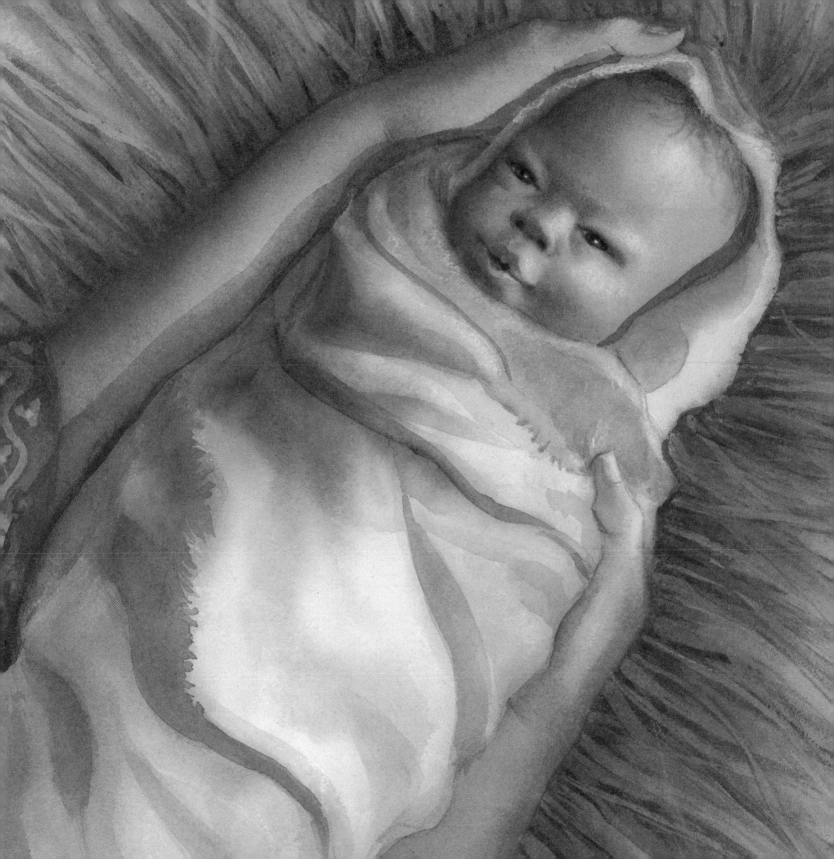

I swaddle you in cloth, safely nestle you in hay.
The sheep and cows are calm as I bow my head and pray.

The precious donkey that brought us safely here
Nuzzles you so softly, sensing God is near.

He has heard the angels blow their trumpets from above
To celebrate your birth and bathe you in their love.

Tomorrow you will be King,

But tonight you are my baby. . . .

Peace and salvation you will bring to all mankind
When others see that you are God's glorious sign.

Among all the people there will be great joy
Upon hearing of you, my dear little boy.

Some will make the journey across the desert sand
To bring you gifts of gold they carry in their hands.

And others will bring music, a simple song to play.
But that is not tonight—it's to be another day.

Tomorrow you will be King,

But tonight you are my baby. . . .

I smile into your loving eyes and give you one more kiss.
This quiet time with you, my son, is what I'm going to miss.

As I sing a peaceful lullaby, you close your eyes to sleep.
This night will be the memory that forever I will keep.

Tomorrow you will be King,

But tonight you are my baby. . . .